Elitism
and the
Spirit of Control
(Control, Manipulation, Spirit of Abortion, Grief and Its Devastating Results)

Kathie Walters

Copyright © 2001 by Kathie Walters
New Expanded Edition 2013
All rights reserved
Printed in the United States of America

International Standard Book Number:
978-1-888081-99-2

Unless otherwise noted, all Scripture quotations are from the New King James Version of the Bible. Copyright © 1979, 1980, 1982 by Thomas Nelson Inc., publishers. Used by permission.

This book or parts thereof may not be reproduced in any form without prior written permission from the

author.

Published by

GOOD NEWS FELLOWSHIP MINISTRIES
220 Sleepy Creek Rd.
Macon, GA 31210
Phone: (478) 757-8071

E-mail: goodnewsministries@usa.com
www.KathieWaltersMinistry.com

Foreword
Who is in Control?

Unfortunately, God's divine order has often been switched to put man in control. In most of the cases the saints that have come under that control have been unaware of the abuse they have suffered by controlling elitist spirits. The extreme "*Shepherding Movement"* that reared its ugly head in the seventies, is still active today in a number of churches. So the question is how and when should we submit to "*delegated"* authority that is taught in the scriptures?

I have taught on this several times over the years and would like to share what I believe to be how God's divine order works.

Scriptural authority is given at different levels and they cannot be switched.

>**1.)** The highest or first level of authority is "***God's Character.***"
>
>**2.)** The second level of authority is the "***Word of God***" or the "***Scriptures.***"

3.) The third level of authority is one's "***Conscience.***"

These are the highest levels and if they stay in that order then all is well.

You might ask isn't the scriptures the highest? No, it's God's character. It is not difficult for some to use (or misuse) the scriptures to destroy or control people. Anything that is taught, or your told to do which is against the character of God is taboo, regardless of who it is that teaches it. Remember Paul said, *"for the letter kills, but the Spirit gives life."* **(2.Cor.3:6)**

The letter of the law brings death. There is no life in laws, rules, religious traditions, or regulations, if they are taught as necessary to have salvation or the blessing of God. So many people obey their leaders without question and yet they have that uneasiness in their hearts that all is not well.

This brings us to the third level which is your conscience. If you are taught something that you don't feel peace in your heart about, or you can't really agree, or accept what's taught and you don't really believe it; but you do it anyway, then you are in sin, and the person or persons that are controlling you are in sin also, because they have caused you to sin. *"For whatever is not of faith is sin."* **(Rom.14:23)**

"But without faith it is impossible to please Him, for whoever comes to God must believe that He is a rewarder of those who diligently seek Him." **(Heb.11.6)**

Number four is Delegated Authority

If delegated authority is put above the first three levels, then control and chaos can become rampant.

4.) Delegated authority is found **in Eph.5:21-24.**

"Submitting to one another in the fear of the Lord."

So first we have a **mutual submission.** Then in that spirit, wives are told to **submit** themselves to their own husbands as to the Lord.

"For the husband is the head of the wife also as Christ is the head of the church; and He is the savior of the body. Therefore, just as the church is subject to Christ, so let the wives be to their own husbands in everything." **(Eph. 5:22-24)**

Now here comes the danger. If a husband starts to imagine that he is the Savior to his wife and her body and believes that forcing **submission** on his wife like a strong wrestler forcing **submission** on a weaker one is perfectly legitimate, then his authority is out of order.

If he believes that he is the only one that hears from God for her and she receives all her spiritual input from her husband, then he is out of order. He must be open to receive the word of the Lord from his wife and even his children. He is then **submitting** to the Spirit of God working in them.

The next scripture tell that a husband must love his wife as Christ loved the church and gave himself for it. If he doesn't, then that negates any authority he may believe he has over her.

For the wife to be willing to **submit** to her husband it is not for her to **submit** to his flesh nature, but to the Spirit of Christ in Him, assuming that is operating in his life. That principle obviously works both ways. (**See Eph.5:21-29**)

Another scripture that can be misused is found in (**1.Pet. 2: 13-14**)

"Therefore submit yourselves to every ordinance of man for the Lord's sake, whether to the king as supreme or to governors, as to those who are sent by him for the punishment of evildoers and for praise of those who do good."

Again, only submit if that doesn't contradict God's character or goes against scripture or destroys your conscience.

Then there is the authority of the elders, pastors or leaders in the church. They cannot and should never force anyone to adhere to church or religious traditions, especially if it offends the members understanding of the word of God or their consciences. The word of God should never be manipulated to favor the leadership and shortchange the average believer. In fact it should be taught to bring the average believer to reach their God given potential and destiny.

Although Paul talks about elders ruling well and be counted as receiving double honor and how they should be given wages for their work, it doesn't mean that they should lord it over the people**. (See 1.Tim.5:17)**

Remember the words of Jesus.

"*You know that those who call themselves rulers over the Gentiles lord it over them and their great ones exercise authority over them. Yet it shall not be so among you; but whoever desires to become great among you shall be your servant. And whoever of you desires to be first shall be the slave of all. For even the Son of Man did not come to be served, but to serve and give His life a ransom for many."* **(Mark.10:42-45)**

I guess that the last on the list of delegated authority is for children submitting.

"Children obey your parents in the Lord, for this is right. Honor your father and mother which is the first commandment with promise: that it may be well with you and you may live long on the earth."

"And you fathers, do not provoke your children to anger, but bring them up in the training and admonition of the Lord." **(Eph.6:1-4)**

Although I list it as last it really is of great importance. For there is a lot of teaching on the subject of parenting. We have books covering that subject on our web book store, but let me say a couple of things.

"Therefore the law was our tutor to bring us to Christ, that we may be justified by faith. But after faith has come we are no longer under a tutor. For you are all children of God through faith in Jesus Christ." **(Gal.3:24-26)**

Our children need to be trained, not merely raised in a Christian home, but trained up in the way they should go, **(See Prov. 22:6)** until faith comes for them. This is not primarily the churches responsibility or the mother's responsibility, but the father's as well as mentioned in **(Eph. 6: 4)**

There is no reason that our children cannot experience all the blessing of salvation and Pentecost and being able to move in the spirit with a sense of destiny and with miracles operating in their lives at a young age, regardless of what your church or others teach.

Many years ago I was preaching at a church in California which was very strong in controlling the people. It was called the *"Discipleship church."* They were very strong on teaching covering. For example;

"Who is your covering?" Who are you under, or submitted to?"

I preached on Sunday morning and the Lord told me to preach on the text.

"Woe unto them that cover with a covering which is not of My Spirit and take counsel, but not of Me." **(Isa. 30:1)**

It set the people free and it was the best Sunday morning that they had experience in ages. But it caused havoc amongst the elders and leaders. Most of them were out of town at the time, but when the heard the tape they chased me across the country, verbally warning people not to have me preach in their churches.

Remember always check and make sure that any authority that is taught to you and which you have received, is in God's divine order.

Enjoy the revelation in Kathie's book and be fed by what she shares.

David Walters.

Introduction

Have you ever been around a church or group and gradually began to feel left out, excluded? Not part of the "*in group*" or inner circle?

What is this exclusiveness or elitism and where did it come from? How did it get there? What opened the door for this to enter? Elitism is a form of pride and the Bible says, *"God resists the proud and gives grace to the humble"* **(James.4:6)**

As Christians, what constitutes humility? True humility is a dependence upon God. Knowing that apart from Him, His power and care, we cannot make it in life or in ministry. We are kept only by His grace.

"Who are kept by the power of God through faith for salvation ready to be revealed in the last time."
(1.Pet.1:3-5)

Warning signs

When an individual or group gives the impression they have some kind of *"special"* calling, or revelation, or when they feel and give the impression they have been called by God to fill some kind of *"special"* place the signals are flashing. The attitude of, *"we are the ones **really** doing the work of the ministry,"* is given out like an offensive odor. Other ministries are deemed as valid, but do not have the great importance *"our"* ministry has.

Often this happens when there has been some kind of success in growth, or a move of God and blessings are manifested. It's often when things are going well, people are not on guard and this exclusive spirit slips in. What begins as a cry of *"GOD is visiting us,"* gradually becomes *"God is VISITING us,"* to finally *"God is visiting US."*

God pours out His Spirit because we are hungry and because we need Him, not because we have *"qualified"* or earned some special favor. He (Jesus) is the One who will present us faultless.

"Now unto Him who is able to keep you from falling and to present you faultless before the presence of His glory with exceeding Joy" **(Jude 24).**

It is the Spirit who changes us

" But we all, with unveiled face, beholding as in a mirror the glory of the Lord, are being transformed into the same image from glory to glory, just as by the Spirit of the Lord" **(2 Cor.3:18).**

"For we are His workmanship, created in Christ Jesus for good works, which God prepared beforehand that we should walk in them" **(Eph. 2:10).**

Unfortunately, in the midst of blessing it seems easy for us to forget it is only because of His great love, grace, mercy, and loving kindness that the blessings came. We begin to feel, with the encouragement of a few demonic forces, that somehow it had something to do with us. Gradually an attitude of resistance emerges against anyone who disagrees with anything the controlling person says or does. Instead of being open to receive input, pride sees anything that is not strongly pro (in agreement with the group or individual) as a threat to their position.

Control and Manipulation

When leaders start to operate in elitism, or become exclusive, they often see others as subjective and inferior to them in some way. Then deception comes in the form of believing that this one person or persons are in a better or more qualified position spiritually to know what is right, or hear from God and know the mind of the Lord. Gradually anyone who questions anything, (decision or teaching etc.) becomes the target of some kind of spiritual attack.

Often accused of being a *"Jezebel"* or *"rebellious."* The person bringing a word or question is dismissed as irrelevant. If that person stands their ground, they are usually rejected, and their own ministry gift questioned, dismissed, and often aborted by the strong religious spirit coming against them.

When a spirit of control comes into a leadership, often the spirit of abortion is active and the move of the Spirit in the church and in the individual is aborted. If that happens, the person involved usually needs prayer for deliverance from the spirit of abortion, and also the spirit of grief.

The False Shepherding Spirit.

The desire to control opens the door to the false shepherding spirit. What exactly is a false shepherding spirit someone may ask? I guess the famous Ezekiel 34 chapter spells it out.

God, the True Shepherd

1 *And the word of the LORD came to me, saying,*

2 *"Son of man, prophesy against the shepherds of Israel, prophesy and say to them, 'Thus says the Lord GOD to the shepherds; "Woe to the shepherds of Israel who feed themselves! Should not the shepherds feed the flocks?"*

3 *"You eat the fat and clothe yourselves with the wool; you slaughter the fatlings, but you do not feed the flock."*

4 *"The weak you have not strengthened, nor have you healed those who were sick, nor bound up the broken, nor brought back what was driven away, nor sought what was lost; but with force and cruelty you have ruled them."*

5 *"So they were scattered because there was no shepherd; and they became food for all the beasts of the field when they were scattered."*

6 *"My sheep wandered through all the mountains, and on every high hill; yes, My flock was scattered over the whole face of the earth, and no one was seeking or searching for them"*

7 *"Therefore, you shepherds, hear the word of the LORD:*

8 *"As I live," says the Lord GOD, "surely because My flock became a prey, and My flock became food for every beast of the field, because there was no shepherd, nor did My shepherds search for My flock, but the shepherds fed themselves and did not feed My flock."*

9 *"Therefore, O shepherds, hear the word of the LORD!*

10 *Thus says the Lord GOD:"Behold, I am against the shepherds, and I will require My flock at their hand; I will cause them to cease feeding the sheep, and the shepherds shall feed themselves no more; for I will*

deliver My flock from their mouths, that they may no longer be food for them."

11 *"For thus says the Lord GOD: "Indeed I Myself will search for My sheep and seek them out."*

12 *"As a shepherd seeks out his flock on the day he is among his scattered sheep, so will I seek out My sheep and deliver them from all the places where they were scattered on a cloudy and dark day."*

13 *"And I will bring them out from the peoples and gather them from the countries, and will bring them to their own land; I will feed them on the mountains of Israel, in the valleys and in all the inhabited places of the country."*

14 *"I will feed them in good pasture, and their fold shall be on the high mountains of Israel. There they shall lie down in a good fold and feed in rich pasture on the mountains of Israel."*

15 *"I will feed My flock, and I will make them lie down," says the Lord GOD.*

16 *"I will seek what was lost and bring back what was driven away, bind up the broken and strengthen that which was sick; but I will destroy the fat and the strong, and feed them in judgment."*

17 *'And as for you, O My flock, thus says the Lord GOD: "Behold, I shall judge between sheep and sheep, between rams and goats."*

18 *"Is it too little for you to have eaten up the good pasture, that you must tread down with your feet the residue of your pasture and to have drunk of the clear waters, that you must foul the residue with your feet?"*

19 *"And as for My flock, they eat what you have trampled with your feet, and they drink what you have fouled with your feet."*

20 *"Therefore thus says the Lord GOD to them: "Behold, I Myself will judge between the fat and the lean sheep."*

21 *"Because you have pushed with side and shoulder, butted all the weak ones with your horns, and scattered*

them abroad, therefore I will save My flock, and they shall no longer be a prey; and I will judge between sheep and sheep."

22 "I will establish one shepherd over them, and he shall feed them--My servant David. He shall feed them and be their shepherd. And I, the LORD, will be their God, and My servant David a prince among them; I, the LORD, have spoken."

23 "I will make a covenant of peace with them, and cause wild beasts to cease from the land; and they will dwell safely in the wilderness and sleep in the woods."

24 "I will make them and the places all around My hill a blessing; and I will cause showers to come down in their season; there shall be showers of blessing."

25 "Then the trees of the field shall yield their fruit, and the earth shall yield her increase. They shall be safe in their land; and they shall know that I am the LORD, when I have broken the bands of their yoke and delivered them from the hand of those who enslaved them."

26 *"And they shall no longer be a prey for the nations, nor shall beasts of the land devour them; but they shall dwell safely, and no one shall make them afraid."*

27 *"I will raise up for them a garden of renown, and they shall no longer be consumed with hunger in the land, nor bear the shame of the Gentiles anymore.*

28 *"Thus they shall know that I, the LORD their God, am with them, and they, the house of Israel, are My people," says the Lord GOD."*

29 *"You are My flock, the flock of My pasture; you are men, and I am your God," says the Lord GOD.'* **(Ezekiel 34)**

The shepherd forgets his real calling, to care and tend and nurture, the flock of God, and begins to only be concerned about his agenda. A harsh spirit comes in usually in the guise of *"doing the will of God"* and the sheep are not loved, comforted or edified. Nor are their gifts and callings *"brought forth."* They are not equipped to do the work of the ministry as commanded in Ephesians 4.

Paul also speaks of the false shepherds in Acts 20. The Apostle exhorts the elders of the Ephesus church,

"Take heed therefore unto yourselves and unto all the flock of which the Holy Ghost has made you overseers, to feed the church of God, which HE HATH PURCHASED WITH HIS OWN BLOOD. ...also of your own selves, shall men arise, speaking perverse things, to draw away disciples after them" **(Acts.20:28-30).**

The true shepherds are called to take authority, and come against that which comes against the sheep to harm them, but this spirit turns it around and the leadership begins to come against the sheep to control and manipulate them. A good shepherd doesn't lead his sheep to a field, pull up grass and ram it down the sheep's throat. He leads them to fresh pasture and they feed themselves. He avails them good food (ministry) and watches out for the sheep.

He sees it as an honor to be given charge among the precious Body of Christ. He can acknowledge the Christ in everyone, even the children and teens, (they do **not** have a junior Holy Spirit) he is not threatened by their gifts and abilities. He will work to bring forth younger men and women and consider it delightful to see them begin to move out in God.

When my husband, David, has miracle meetings, God begins to use the children and teens, who come under his anointing He sits down and God's Spirit uses them. Miracles happen through *"the laying on of sticky fingers"* as David calls it. He loves to see God use the youngsters in such a powerful way. It is life changing for them, as well as those who receive healing. So is the heart of the true shepherd.

Misuse of God- given Authority

I was once involved with a group of powerful evangelistic churches. The leader of this group was a man of great vision and faith. But he became very verbally abusive in his role of leader, and extremely controlling.

People really did not have the opportunity to hear from God for themselves and be led by the Spirit. A kind of *"dictator"* type spirit manifested toward the people.

Those who disagreed were branded as *"rebellious"* or *"Jezebels"* and accused of not having a submissive spirit.

When you come under a false shepherding spirit, you also end up needing deliverance from a spirit of false submission. True submission is not a matter of just blindly doing whatever you are told. It means that you are open to others, that God may speak to you through whomever He wishes, especially a loving, caring shepherd. And, always being open to the fact that something may need to be corrected, in your direction, or your walk with God.

As people learn to yield to the Spirit, God will fit them into the right place in the Body of Christ, and the true shepherds of Jesus can help them to fulfill their destiny.

The Lord gave me a word for the leader of this group of churches. I wasn't at all willing to bring it.

"Who do you think you are?" said a voice in my ear. You know what? I'm not anyone, I'm an **"are not."** But God has chosen the the things that *"are not"* hasn't He?

"But God has chosen the foolish things of the world to put to shame the wise and God has chosen the weak things of the world to put to shame the things which are mighty; and the base things of the world and the things which are despised God has chosen, and the things which are not, to bring to nothing the things that are, that no flesh should glory in His presence" **(1 Cor. 1: 27- 29).**

Reluctantly, I delivered this word to a leadership meeting in which it was read out. *"You have one year to rid the ministry of the of the false shepherding spirit."* That's all it was, so I left it there. When God gives you a word, it's not your responsibility to make it happen, it's His. I continued to fellowship with this group and didn't think too much more about it.

A year later at the same annual leadership meeting, the whole ministry began to become unglued. Three months later it was out of action and no longer existed as an entity. God removed the rod of authority, because it was being misused and hurt the sheep.

"Touch not My anointed and do My prophets no harm"
(Psalms 105:15)

This is very often quoted with regard to leadership people as a way of saying, *"Leave me alone you have no right to question me or my decisions."* But the *"anointed"* spoken of in the Psalm, also includes the whole Body of Christ; that's everyone, including you and I.

The elitist spirit ensures that leaders forget that every believer has the capability of hearing from God and being used by Him. A child filled with God's Spirit can be used in a mighty way. That's why it's so important to be open to anyone in the Body. God can use whoever He desires.

The Life of Christ is deposited in each member. What is the responsibility of the members towards the leadership? To care for them, pray for them, help, encourage and work with them. Knowing that God has called them to help His people be equipped for the Kingdom and be ministered to, enabling the church to be healthy.

*"...But speaking the truth in love, may grow up in all things into Him who is the head - Christ, from whom the whole body, joined and knit together by **what every joint supplies,** according to the effective working by which every part does its share, causes growth of the body for the edifying of itself in love"* **(Eph. 4:15-16).**

You have the witness of the Spirit inside you, to teach you. It is ultimately your own responsibility to put yourself under godly men and women and receive teaching and instruction that comes from God which is really from the Word. Biblical grounding is important. But it must be also have the Holy Spirit's anointing. Remember what Paul said,

"Who also made us sufficient as ministers of the new covenant, not of the letter but of the Spirit; for the letter kills, but the spirit gives life" **(2 Cor.3:6).**

Sometimes I admit I get a little impatient with people who have sat under control, deception, false shepherding for a long time. They are in a big mess, but when I question them, they say sat there in some church or ministry knowing inside that something was wrong, (that's the witness of the Spirit). Instead of checking it out they just sat there and got deeper into it.

If you feel the Lord gives you something for the church or leadership, present it humbly, (you could be wrong!). If the leadership is godly they will consider what you have, but you must leave it with them.

God once put me in a position where I had to pray for many people who came out of a group who were operating in a false shepherding/discipleship spirit. These were young Christians being trained and discipled by a man who was obviously anointed for evangelism - he did get them saved and dedicated to God. The success of the group went to his head and he began to put pressure on these young men and women.

"If you really want to serve God you must do what I say, as I am your father (teacher) sent by God to be over you." Then came, *"You must do as I say - it is a test of your willingness to obey God."*

You can guess where it ended up; he eventually had sex with most of the young women. And then sent young single women to live with married couples to be *"discipled."* Really they were servants. I talked to one or two young women who had been told that part of the discipleship was to learn about how to be a good sexual partner for their future husband. Guess how? Of course the husband in the home they were living was told it was his *"duty"* to teach them (in a practical way)!! When we got round to praying deliverance for these people, we prayed for the following and they got free.

Elitism, false shepherding, false submission, false covering, false yoke, false responsibility, control, witchcraft, false brotherhood, bands (the group gets yoked together with a band that isn't from God, they become a *"family."* Fear, fear of disapproval, rejection, grief, abortion (they were not allowed to operate in any spiritual gifts) guilt, shame, condemnation. False martyr spirit (suffering wrong doing for Jesus). This spirit told people that they just had to put up with all this unpleasantness as they were being sacrificed for the kingdom. In this group, as in many others like it, there were a lot of other kinds of deception taught. i.e. *"If you really love someone and want them to be healed, you will pray for their sickness to come to you so they can be free from it."* Spirits of deception, unfruitfulness, barrenness, dead works, etc. Are there really all these spirits involved? Yes there certainly are. They roam around like a little army, each one in position to take over. These folks were not set free until we had broken the power of all these things. I believe everything would have been discovered much sooner if the gifts of the Spirit were flowing.

Then a deaf and dumb spirit comes in, as they are not allowed to hear from God for themselves and certainly not allowed to speak up.

The first spirit to enter is **elitism or pride.** That is why it is so **important to watch** out for these things.

". . lest Satan should take advantage of us; for we are not ignorant of his devices" **(2 Cor.2:11).**

But sadly, so often we **are** ignorant and God's people have **not** been taught to listen to the witness of the Spirit. That's why the anointing is there within us, the believer. It is to teach us. Please read these scriptures, they are so important for us all.

"And this is the promise that He has promised us, eternal life. These things have I written to you concerning those who try to deceive you, But the anointing which you have received from Him abides in you, and you do not need that any man teach you: but as the same anointing teaches you concerning all things, and is true, and is not a lie and just as it has taught you, you will abide in Him. And now little children, abide in Him, that when He appears, we may have confidence, and not be ashamed before Him at His coming. If you know that He is righteous, you know that everyone who practices righteousness is born of Him" **(I. John 2:25-29).**

Does this mean that we no longer need teachers and instructors? Of course not! Paul urges Timothy **(2.Tim.4:2)** to teach and preach, be instant in season and out of season. He exhorts him to teach sound doctrine. This means that when we receive teaching we must still watch the witness of the spirit within us.

If you understand how these spirits operate, you can pray and get free; you do not have to *"qualify"* to receive from God. I would encourage you to listen several times to my CD *"Getting Free and Living in the Supernatural."* It talks about the three main religious spirits that prevent you from receiving everything that God has for you. The qualifying spirit, false responsibility and false burdens. You can order or download from my website.

A Note for Pastors and Leaders:

This booklet is intended for people who have been abused by authority in the church. As you are aware there have been many leaders who have misused their position in the church and misrepresented the true leadership that is God appointed. Unfortunately many of these wounded sheep are not yet healed, but God is touching and restoring them and giving them understanding of the spiritual realm.

I am aware that there are people that do not want to listen to anyone, but I am not addressing those people.

Testimony from Faith Walters

When I first realized where my life had come, I didn't know how I ended up there. I only knew that I somehow managed to do so. And it wasn't long after, that I found I wasn't the only one who had this experience. But before I can tell you where I had ended up, I must tell you where I started out.

I was saved at 4 years old and continued my life (not just my childhood, but all my adult years as well) in church, serving the church, serving God. I have in the past, been part of many church endeavors and more *"moves of God"* than I can remember, and an ocean full of *"waves of the Spirit."*

I considered myself a charismatic, non-religious, world changer and history maker. Everything from cutting edge rock worship music, to market place ministry, to the jungles of Africa, cell groups, prophetic art, dancing, power evangelism and everything in between. My family and the people we surrounded ourselves with, were Holy Spirit shakers, lovers of God and on-fire radicals living, breathing and doing the Gospel. Or so was my perception of things.

I loved going to church, especially my church. I loved being a part of a community of believers that shared the same vision and goals as we did! A place that broke barriers, pushed boundaries, prophesied, preached, prayed, worshiped with abandonment, equipped their people, healed the sick, and even had an instance of raising the dead. This was it! We had arrived.

Of course, there were some things, circumstances, teachings and such that popped up here and there that brought an uncertainty, a dissatisfaction, but all was quickly justified by Scripture and wise counsel. Those in authority, knew best and were readily able to prove it so. But after some time passed and I found myself, once arrayed in the luminescence of radiant ministry, now left fumbling around an odd smoke-filled dinginess, trying to find my way through, or out or around. Thus began my journey to find God.

I have coined the term before describing this part of my life as both a *"systems failure"* and also a *"spiritual eclipse."* Because in essence, both happened. And it took the first to bring about the second.

Most of us have had something happen in our lives, something big, something that shakes you to your core and blows your mind totally out of whack. And when this happened to me, I found myself in a place of like a great eclipse in mind, soul and spirit. I watched as my very life, my very heart, my whole world, my core belief system went into a giant systems failure. And there I was, not even sure why or how it happened in the first place.

For a long time I thought it was a specific instance that brought me to this place. Often terrible things like death, divorce, bankruptcy etc. initiate a crossing place in our lives. But really, when I looked deeper, it was not the calamity, in my case a divorce, that brought me to a place of spiritual degeneration or awakening; it depends on your perception as to which you would call it. I call it an eclipse. It was churchianity that essentially brought me to this place. Divorce just added the fuel to the fire, that I didn't realized had already started to slowly ignite.

In some small ways, I had long been to rocking the boat. I would very passively challenge things that didn't sit right; teachings or beliefs etc. But I managed to let myself be talked out of what I was feeling inside. That witness of the Spirit in me, was quieted and pushed aside and I eventually found myself under control in many areas... and I didn't even realize some of them until I was out from under them. Control can be extremely sneaky.

My personality is first a co-operator and then an analyzer. So I always had a battle going on within me. But because I wanted to keep the peace at all costs, the co-operator side always won in the end and I gave into things whether I agreed with them or not. At the time I didn't realize that this was spiritual abuse and manipulation. And it was easily used against me because of my peace-keeping personality and good nature. It something worked like this:

The times when I was doing things I didn't want to do, I was told that if I didn't, I was disobeying the Lord or His Word. And that in disobeying the Lord, I was stepping out of His *"umbrella of grace"* and bad things could happen to me. When I tried to speak out about wrongs being done to me, I was told I have a *"victim spirit "* and needed to be delivered from it. When I expressed concerns about things in my life, marriage and at home that were not changing for the better, I was told it was because I had unforgiveness and bitterness and it was stopping the Lord from working. Now I am not saying that this can not sometimes be true, but it was not true with me. It was spiritual manipulation and control over me, but how did I end up letting others have so much control over me? It was misplaced faith.

Misplaced faith is the key factor in the perceived de-evolvement (and ultimately you can look back and see it was really an evolvement) of one's relationship with God. It gives you a distorted view of who God is. It causes you to try to earn God's approval…. but it can be very sneaky. We all may say, *"YES, God loves us all!"* but in the back of our minds we think things like:

"The reason this bad thing is happening to me, is because I must have done something wrong (God is punishing me ,) " or even more subtly, *God's blessings are blocked , because of a sin in my life. I will be more blessed the more I please God (which is by doing something - like tithing, giving, joining a ministry, making some sort of self-sacrifice, have enough faith, etc.)"*

Other misplaced faith ideas we hold on to include very common thoughts like:

"If I really have faith, that person would be healed."

"The more money I sow, the more blessings I get in return."

"I must submit to authority over me in order to be right with God or to please God."

"Real faith keeps away problems and pain."

"To truly trust in God, means He does everything and I do nothing (as in, I don't go to work, because I fully trust God an He will provide everything)."

"I am just a sinner, unworthy of God's forgiveness."

Misplaced faith will cause 1 plus 1 to not equal 2. How do we comprehend when we have "done everything right", yet things don't turn out like we were promised? In my life, the effect did not equal the cause. And it began to be more than I could bear. It didn't happen right away, it took two, three, four or more times before it became too much. But I unknowingly continued to misplace my faith, and not get the return I was expecting, and it frustrated me to no end.

Some who have gone through the same situation have gotten fed up and left God altogether, and others have just tried harder, constantly worried about what they are doing wrong and gradually becoming angry, afraid or, disillusioned. Or like me, letting myself be put under control because maybe someone else has the answer I couldn't seem to grasp for myself. Any and all of these responses can end up sabotaging your relationship with God.

I remember on numerous occasions, *"having faith"* for our finances. This is such a tricky, gray area. But it seemed, no matter which way I tried to *"have faith"* for money, our big financial breakthrough never happened. I can look back now and see that my misplaced faith, generated a cause and effect attitude in me towards this and other situations as well. Another instance was my marriage. For years and years I *"did all the right things."*

I forgave, I submitted, I prayed, I counseled with the pastors... but the marriage didn't heal and the change needed didn't take place.

I have observed that this misplaced faith can be quite toxic. It eats away at us, at our relationship with Him, at our worth and righteousness. We begin to feel we have failed in some way. Done something wrong. At least this is how I ended up feeling most of the time. And this is NOT what God wants for us. But because I didn't know how to change it myself, I put my trust in men, who then used my vulnerability to control me.

Control comes in many forms; outright control we usually instantly recognize. When a person is controlling in a violent way, its obvious to everyone. But the captivating controller is another creature entirely. Usually this person is a pastor, husband or elder or someone in *"authority."* That's who they were to me. People whom I thought I could trust. But instead, taking advantage of my misplaced faith, Mr. Super-Spirituals (we shall call them and I use plural because it is often more than one person) used that to produce an action in me that benefited him and the church.

Through my (misplaced) faith and using Scripture and the prophetic "word of the Lord," Mr. Super-Spirituals gained my trust and my loyalty. I belonged, was accepted, was loved... as long as I paid my tithe, attended the prayer meeting/outreach, obeyed my spiritual heads, agreed with the teachings and didn't stir up anything among the congregation.

And this went for everyone else too, not just me. Anyone could be equipped for ministry, teach classes, be on the worship team, but just make sure you don't question anything and stay in the slot given to you...because that's how the wheels continuously turn so smoothly. So don't make things get bumpy, by getting out of your place.

Sometimes church members were even discouraged from receiving teaching or impartation from other ministries besides the pastor or pastor approved ministries. This is because Mr. Super-Spirituals was afraid someone might receive something that rocked the boat.

I remember getting a phone call one time that concerned an invite that I emailed out. I was organizing a girls night out and invited many of my friends from different areas around the city. On the other line was a Mr.

Super-Spirituals (actually this one was a Mrs.), who began to question me about a certain friend that was included in the email.

This certain friend had once been part of my church at the time, but had since moved on as they felt the Lord lead them to go elsewhere. I was admonished for inviting this certain friend to my girls night out, since they were no longer part of the church and then I was directed to no longer be in communication with this friend.

Another time I received a phone call because someone had gotten wind that I was conducting a personal study of some Scriptures using the Source New Testament as a reference. Now, understand this, I was personally studying this, not even a cell group study or study with a few friends. A personal one. But revelation I was receiving was considered to be boat-rocking revelation. So interrogations began and I was admonished for using study material Mr. Super-Spirituals did not deem to be appropriate for me to use. I was made to feel less than for thinking differently, which caused me to give in, for a time, to Mr. Super-Spiritual's demands. How did they managed to do that?

I had seen everything from name calling, to ridiculing and mocking to slander and gossiping and even a modern version of excommunication. All because someone didn't agree doctrinally, or didn't follow some regulations they were told they needed to achieve, or did not acquiesce to a teaching that was served up on a Sunday morning. I saw the pain and humiliation people were put through. Or in some cases, the gossip and lies spoken about them after their departure. I did not want that to be me.

Another scenario that can happen in the control mode can be the disuniting of families and friends. This happened to me for a period of time when I was "rocking the boat" a little too much. Mr. Super-spirituals began to feel threatened, began to feel their *"place of authority"* was threatened, so they sought to disunite me with everyone who did not agree with them: or with who they felt might influence me in another way than they sought to influence me.

You may see this same thing around you subtly at first: joking about the persons beliefs; like in laughing and saying something to the effect of, *"how can they believe that!"* or *"I can't believe they actually think that!"* Or possibly having an attitude of *"well, when they grow up spiritually a bit more, they will understand then."* Mr. Super-Spirituals tries to keep their illusion of authority by making themselves look well relative and full of understanding, and like the other person hasn't arrived at that place yet in their spiritual growth.

So then you feel less spiritual if you agree with the other person! If the one who feels their hold over you is threatened enough, they may even cause you to end a friendship or disconnect with a family member or members. This happened to me and I was not allowed to contact my family for a period of almost three months. This is very painful and hurtful not only to us, but to the Lord. This is the farthest thing from His heart.

Some people actually function well under control then they don't have to think for themselves, or be responsible for making decisions. It can be a relief to some people, because they no longer have to worry that they are doing the right thing, or correctly following the ways of the Lord. They shift the responsibility for their life from themselves to the person who is deemed as in authority over them.

This is most common with wives to their husbands, but is also rampant with congregations to their pastors.

Firstly, no one can have the responsibility of telling us what the Lord would have us do or be and then making sure we submit to it. We no longer live in the day of the priest. The veil was ripped open as part of the work of the cross. Someone being your *"priest"* takes your faith off of Jesus' work on the cross and onto a person: your faith becomes misplaced.

Secondly, there is no person who is greater in the spirit than another, or over, or more spiritual, or in authority over another person.

This kind of *"church government"* is not a New Testament idea. It is an idea that developed later in the centuries during the time Catholicism was taking shape. 1 Cor. 12 plainly tells us that ALL gifts, ALL ministries are given by the same God and worked through the same Holy Spirit and that no gift or ministry is more important or greater than another. Galatians tells us that in the spirit, there is no Jew nor Greek, slave nor free, male nor female.

We are all the same in Christ Jesus. And Matt 20 goes so far as to make sure we know that ruling over one another in the body of Christ, is not the way Jesus has for us.

We are all joint heirs with Jesus. We, ourselves, are all solely responsible for our own thoughts, actions, beliefs, not for anyone else or anyone else for us. Elders and deacons (and now what we call the pastor) in the church are supposed to be there to uplift, facilitate, equip, encourage and offer counsel. Not be the boss or the bully. Titus 3 is referring to obeying governmental leaders and the laws of the land. And even in that, we should never obey anything that contradicts the Nature of God, the Word of God or the witness of the Spirit within us (or our conscience).

You can only find yourself under control, if you have misplaced your faith. Put your faith back in the right position and you remove yourself out from under control.

It wasn't until my divorce that that the ground shook, so to speak. And it shook me right out of the church, and almost out of my mind.

Most who have experienced what I have been talking about, haven't stuck around long enough to witness this next devastating spectacle. This is the one that can destroy families, relationships, lives, hearts and dreams.

That "circumstance" we talked about earlier, can bring such a negative response from the church, that this is the time the aforementioned spiritual eclipse is most likely to take place. In my case, divorce was the catapult that flung my life into a series of injurious events, a system failure and ultimately into a spiritual eclipse.

Actually, let me correct that statement... it was the final breakdown of an already contravened marriage that was the catalyst.

The reaction to my situation from my beloved fellow believers and spiritual leaders had the opposite effect they were hoping for. In truth, the hardness and harshness directed at me actually helped to pilot my conclusion to finally flee. Because by then, I had to flee to be free.

The reaction I was awarded for my pain, despair and confusion of an ending marriage, was one of self preservation on their part.

My misplaced faith, in faith itself, led me to a place of unhealthy submission. But when my faith (if I did all the things I was supposed to: forgive, let go, be healed, change, submit and pray) did not give me the promised outcome (my marriage would be healed, restored and renewed), I become a liability to the peace and function of the great ministry machine, instead of a reliable, well oiled, ever-turning wheel in that machine of church life and ministry.

This self-preservation (church preservation, congregation preservation etc) actuates the quick discarding of liabilities. And I had become a liability. I lost not only my marriage, but my whole life-blood ministry and community of close-knit friends, families and loved ones. If my parents, my sister and a teeny tiny handful of a loving, compassionate (non church) few hadn't have been there for me, I do not know what would have become of me.

After being put through horrendous trials and tests of my faith, loyalty, forgiveness, being remorseful, and submissiveness, I was still found wanting.

In the midst of an ending marriage, I was sent to live for a week with a *"model family"* and learn from the wife how to be *"the wife God called me to be"* in hopes I would model my marriage after theirs.

I completed all the tasks and goals I was given that promised me a saved marriage, but to no avail. I was told that even I did everything and nothing changed with my husband or marriage, it would be "*counted to me for righteousness.*" I pointed out that someone had already given me some righteousness His name was Jesus!

I ended up being cut off, turned out, rejected and ejected from the place I once thought I was most accepted. And I had gossip, slander and malice follow me for a long time after. I was publicly excommunicated and my best friends never spoke to me again. The shunning spirit is a wicked spirit.

So I found my self at this place of eclipse. My system failure had taken place and everything I knew to be good, true, holy, and just was suddenly ripped away. I was left with two ideas only.

Is this really how God is? A mean con artist? Is He really someone that would present me a deal (or contract), require me to hold up my end of the bargain and then sometimes not hold up His end? And then when brought to His attention, would justify His behavior by blaming my lack of faith? This thought outraged me. I suddenly became filled with compassion for those people labeled *"rebellious"* out there!

Rebellion is a vastly overused Christianized word that many lazy and blame shifting people use when they don't want to take responsibility for leading others in misplaced faith. They are really just people who have recognized misplace faith and control for what it is and bailed before self-preservation kicked in.

Was I being shown God through various teachings, ministries and people, giving me a gross misrepresentation of who He really is?

And so I began the journey that I am still on today. I have discovered particulars along the way, some I have liked and some I haven't. Some about God and some about people. But the best thing I have discovered is God's love.

Galatians has been my anchor. Get out of your dusty mind box and read it, not in the KJV or the NIV, but in the Message or the Source.... there is a reason these translations were named liked they are. I still don't have all the answers to my own questions, or know exactly what I think about every doctrinal issue. But I do know one thing; God's love is simple and never-ending. His love doesn't require anything out of you. His approval doesn't come from anything you do.... it comes from what He did. We negate the great work of the cross, by doing something to earn anything from God. When the Bible says in Heb. 11,*"without faith, it is impossible to please God"* . It doesn't mean faith to work miracles or faith to have enough money. It is talking about the faith it takes to believe that what happened on the cross was enough; that there is nothing more to do. We are received, accepted, loved, treasured, approved of and qualified for just by believing we are.

Everyone should tuck 1 Cor. 13 deep down in the heart. Memorize it, speak it, live it. The *"power"* versus come just before in 1 Cor. 12. They speak of gifts, ministries, power, the body of Christ. But so many forget the short but ultra-powerful statement that bridges chapter 12 to 13: *"And now I show you a more excellent way."* And that way is love. Because all of chapter 12 doesn't mean a single solitary thing without chapter 13. I adore how The Message puts this verse... *"So, no matter what I say, what I believe, and what I do, I'm bankrupt without love."*

Recently I heard someone say that the reason they were on the earth was to teach and preach, save the lost and heal the sick. This sounds very noble and spiritual... but its not true. It's a sign of misplaced faith. We were created and put on this earth to enjoy God, the world he gave us, be loved by Him and be in relationship with Him.

When we believe that our purpose in life is to do works, then we begin to have a works mentality. We may start off doing these works because we want to serve the Lord (and that's great), but if we aren't careful, soon our faith is placed in the works, rather than in God. They become compulsory, and you even come to a place where you feel ashamed that you did not preach to the lady in the store, or pray for that person to be healed, read your devotional that day. Then fear enters. Fear that God is upset with you, or disappointed in you, and now your car broke down because of it. If there is a controlling authority over you, they will use this to further their ministry, by getting you to spin your wheel in the machine even harder, to *"fulfill your destiny"* and please God.

The movie *"The Matrix"* has been used by many as a parable for becoming a Christian... when you were in the world, you were asleep, existing in a false reality (natural world), and when you get saved, your eyes are opened and you are awakened to the real world (spiritual world).

Though I can see truth in this, it can again be a misplaced faith that will lead you away from God's love and not towards it. In this movie, Neo, who is awakened to the real world, goes through a series of tests and conflicts, some he wins, some he looses, until when he has done enough, believed enough, he finally arrives at a place of magnificent destiny and power.

Sounds inspiring, doesn't it? But be careful here; trial, conflict, tests, are not given for us to pass and become a greater, more loved, more powerful Christian. Passing them does not grant us special sanctions from God to be able to preform greater feats of spirituality. Neither does fasting, I might mention.

So when you make it through some difficult times, and you don't suddenly have (or see) the breakthrough in your finances, or the healing in your body, or become a super-Christian, it is not because you didn't have enough faith, it is because you have misplaced your faith.

When you've done all that your leaders (or husband) requires, been faithful, been submissive, but the miracle you've been praying for still doesn't come through, you have just been submitting to pointless and often damaging control through misplaced faith. Faith is believing God and what He has done. Real faith, takes the pressure off, not adds more on.

You might at this point ask, how do I have faith then for finances, healing, miracles? There isn't a formula to give you. It's just simple faith in a simple Gospel. We over think and over complicate things so much, that it is more difficult for us to just simply have simple faith than an intricate set of rules and delicate balance we desperately, (but failingly) try to live.

If you begin this journey like I have, be prepared. Prepared for people to call you crazy, call you rebellious and question all of your choices and decisions. People will "pray and intercede" for you and may even call, write or email you teachings, Bible versus, and their 2 cents. It is nature (unfortunately) for people to jump to conclusions, believe the worst, gossip and *"think they know something"* when they really don't get it at all. Take it all with a grain of salt and continue seeking the Jesus you are looking for.

I love Gal 5:6... *"The only thing that counts, is faith expressing itself through love"*. It has become my motto. It sums up so clearly and simply what our lives are about. To understand anything else the Bible has to say about faith or love, we need to first understand this verse. So that's my journey, to understand and live this verse. Because everything else comes from that. And no matter what you believe, what denomination you are, what religion you are, or no religion at all, I think we can all agree that what counts is *"faith expressing itself through love."*

About the Walters Family

David and Kathie Walters are originally from England. They have lived and ministered in the United States since 1976. The presently reside in Macon, Georgia. They have two daughters, two grandsons and one granddaughter.

David has a burden for families and what he terms church-wise kids and teens, those who have been brought up in the church and have head knowledge of the things of God. His desire is for the young people to have a dynamic experience of God for themselves. His *"Holy Spirit Revival Encounters"* for the whole family including Children/Teens/Students, Pastors, Youth & Children's Pastors, Nursery Workers, Teachers, Parents, Grandparents and Single Adults. He also holds revival meetings for churches and includes the children and teens in the miracle ministry of the Holy Spirit.

David ministers to the whole family and is known by many as an Apostolic Grand Father. He has been on National Television such TBN, and *"It's Supernatural"* with Sid Roth of *"Messianic Vision."* Radio. He has taught at several Bible Colleges including *"Christ For the Nations"* In Dallas Texas. He has also authored sixteen books.

Kathie ministers nationally and internationally at churches, conferences, and woman's retreats. She has been on *"Its Supernatural"* TV program several times with Sid Roth of *"Messianic Vision"* Kathie shows how to live in the supernatural realm of the Holy Spirit. Kathie believes that the miraculous realm is our inheritance. She teaches how to be released from religious mindsets which have kept God's people from their spiritual inheritance.

Kathie ministers not only to women, but often to the whole family. She has spoken at Woman's Aglow, Women of the Word, and Charisma Woman's Conferences. She has ministered with Dr. Fuchsia

Pickett, Iverna Tompkins and many well known teachers and ministers.

Kathie has a special place in her heart for women and encourages them to let their gifts and callings come forth under the anointing of the Holy Spirit. She believes there are many powerful ministries hidden in God's women, and this is the time for their release. Kathie has authored fourteen books and has many sets of great teaching CD's.

Books Available
By Kathie Walters

Angels - Watching over You - Did you know that Angels are very active in our everyday lives?

Celtic Flames - Discover the exciting accounts of other famous Fourth & Fifth Century Celtic Christians: Patrick, Brendan, Cuthbert, Brigid and others.

Columba - The Celtic Dove - Read about the prophetic and miraculous ministry of this famous Celtic Christian, filled with supernatural visitations.

Living in the Supernatural - Kathie believes that the supernatural realm, the angels, miracles, and signs and wonders are the spiritual inheritance of every believer, as in the early church. She tells how to embrace and enter our inheritance.

Parenting - by the Spirit - Kathie shows how she raised her children by listening to the Holy Spirit rather than her emotions.

The Visitation - An account of two heavenly visitations which Kathie experienced. One lasted for seven days and the other for 3 1/2 weeks. Her daughter Faith, also had a visitation when she was just 17 years old.

Seers List – A Biblical list of Prophetic Seers and the Prophetic Seer Ministry today.

Health Related Mindsets – Explanation of mindsets which can bring sickness.

The Spirit of False Judgment—Dealing with Heresy Hunters. Sometimes things are not what they appear to be.

Kathie's CD teaching sets

Getting Free and Living in the Supernatural

David's Mighty Men

Faith and Angels

In Depth for Seers and Prophets

Revival Account and Getting Your Family Saved

Spiritual Strategies

The Almond Tree

The Fanatic in the Attic

The Spirit of Abortion

Books Available
By David Walters

Kids in Combat - David shows how to train children and teens in spiritual power and bring them into the anointing for ministry. (Parents, teachers and children/youth pastors).

Equipping the Younger Saints - Teaching children and youth Salvation, the Baptism of the Holy Spirit and Spiritual gifts (Parents, teachers, children/youth pastors).

Children Aflame - Supernatural accounts of children from the journals of the great Methodist preacher John Wesley in the 1700's and David's own accounts with children and youth.

The Anointing and You/Understanding Revival - How to receive, sustain, impart, and channel the Anointing for renewal/revival, and to pass it onto the next generation.

Radical Living in a Godless Society

Our children and youth are facing onslaughts from our secular, liberal, society. What must the church and parents do to unsure our children won't become casualties in this spiritual war?

So You Think You Know About Worship? - A new radical revelation of worship. A must for worshipers and worship leaders.

Living In Revival (*The Everyday lifestyle of the Normal Christian*)

An amazing account of a Revival that David and Kathie experienced in the early seventies in England. A must for hungry believers.

CHILDREN'S ILLUSTRATED BIBLE STUDY BOOKS

Armor of God - Children's illustrated Bible study on Ephesians 6:14-18 (ages 6-12 years).

Fruit of the Spirit - Children's illustrated Bible study on Galatians 5:22 (ages 6-adults).

Fact or Fantasy - Children's illustrated Bible study on Christian Apologetics. How to defend your faith. (ages 8- adults).

Being a Christian - A Children's illustrated Bible study on what it really means to be a Christian (ages 7- adults).

Children's Prayer Manual - Children's Illustrated study on prayer (ages 6-14 years).

The Gifts of the Spirit - Children's Illustrated Bible study on the Gifts (ages 8- adults).

How to be Ordinary, Mediocre, Average and Unsuccessful — A very amusing reverse psychology booklet.

David Also Has Several Fun Adventure Books For Children.

The Book of Funtastic Adventures - David's two grandsons have amazing hilarious adventures as imaginary junior Jedi Knights.

The 2nd Book of Funtastic Adventures - More hilarious adventures of the two grandsons and their sister.

The Adventures of Tiny the Bear - A cute funny story of how two bears deal with children suffering from bullying and teasing.

TOURS OF IRELAND AND SCOTLAND

with Kathie Walters

Come to Ireland and Scotland on a 14-Day Celtic Heritage Tour with Kathie Walters!

• Pray on the Hill of Slane where St. Patrick lit his Pascal fire and defied the High King.

• See the place where St. Patrick first landed to bring the Gospel to Ireland by God through the Angel of Ireland, Victor.

• See the green hills and dales of Ireland—
  a picture you will never forget.

• Visit the ancient places of worship that will help enable you to grasp hold of your godly inheritance.

Then on to Scotland

• Tour the beautiful highlands of Scotland.

• Visit the island of Iona, where St. Columba built his monastery.

See beautiful Loch Ness and Loch Lomond and visit Edinburgh

Made in the USA
San Bernardino, CA
02 May 2014